Then and Now

By Jenny Vaughan

CELEBRATION PRESS
Pearson Learning Group

Then

Long ago London looked like this.

Now

Today London looks like this.

Then

Yesterday the duckling looked like this.

Now

Today the duckling looks like this.

Then

Last week the flowers looked like this.

Now

Today the flowers look like this.

Then

Last month the play area looked like this.

Now

Today the play area looks like this.

Then

Three months ago the crayons looked like this.

Now

Today the crayons look like this.

Then

Last year the house looked like this.

Now

Today the house looks like this.

Then

Five years ago Damask looked like this.

Now

Today Damask looks
like this.

What will you look like in five years?